The Secret Language of River

Poems

Also by Toni Thomas:

Chosen
Fast as Lightening
Walking on Water
Blue Halo
Ace Raider of the Unfathomable Universe
You'll be Fast as Lightning Coveting my Painted Tail
Hotsy Totsy Ballroom
Love Adrift in the City of Stars
In the Pink Arms of the City
In the Kingdom of Longing
The Things We Don't Know
In the Boarding House for Unclaimed Girls
They Became Wing Perfect and Flew
Unburdened Kisses
Bandits Come and Remove Her Body in the Night
There is This
Here
The Smooth White Vanishing
Perishing in the Rain
A Different Measure of Moonlight
Inside Her a River of Snow was Traveling
In Her Soul the Pale Rooms of the Moon were Wandering

The Secret Language of River

Poems

First published in 2024 by Annalese Press
134 Towngate
Netherthong
Holmfirth
West Yorkshire HD9 3XZ
England

Copyright © 2013 Toni Thomas
Publication 2024

*All characters and situations appearing
in these pages are creatures of the imagination and in the
service of poetry.
Any resemblance to real persons
living or dead, is purely coincidental.*

All rights reserved. No part of this publication may be reproduced, stored, or transmitted in any form, or by any means electronic, mechanical or photo-copying, recording or otherwise, without the express written permission of the publisher.

Cover design and layout by Peter Wadsworth
Girl with Hat, Amedeo Modigliani, 1918

British Library Cataloguing-in-Publication Data
A catalogue record for this book is available on request from the British Library.

ISBN 978-1-7394457-8-2

Contents

Part One   *The Mute Languor of Snow Falling*

You are tall	3
The child under the woodpile	4
She deals in twin sets	5
She bakes cake in the snow	6
In her hands wander blue ponies	7
She sits like a bent tree	8
She watches you	9
If she shrinks small	11
The girl who always wanted	13
Up the valley	15

Part Two   *A Paragraph in a Sad Hotel*

We weren't worried	19
After the early diagnosis	20
They were getting to know each other	22
She is playing with light	23
The air is steamy	24
Sepia morning	25
It is winter	26
Vermont	27
She doesn't want to ride a dead pony	28
She remembers the woods	29
In her dream she herds sheep	31

Part Three   *Uncompromised Heaven
              on a Shoestring*

When death started to move unrelenting   35
It was done   36
She stick stirs the river   37
You navigate her heart   38
You mouth her words   39
The months of winter   40
She lives in your shroud and wake   41
Mustela Vison   42
In winter   43
Are all roads good roads   44
She is entering a castle   45

Part Four   *The Quiet Disaster of Things*

She has scalded hands   49
In the sleepy hollow of Braithwaite   50
No wooden marker   52

Part Five   *Blue Halo*

For how many years   55
You spot clean winter   56
For you   57
There are furrows of blue bells   58
The retrieval of winter   59

Thank you for loving	60
She twines ribbon	61
She wears silky stockings	62

Part Six   *The Bells*

Who says the angels must	65
In the ordinary course of her days	67
She slides into her amber coat	68

I want to think again of dangerous and noble things
I want to be light and frolicsome
I want to be improbably beautiful and afraid of nothing -
as though I had wings.
Mary Oliver

Bring me the sunset in a cup.
Emily Dickinson

Part One

The Mute Languor of Snow Falling

You are tall

I call you my *green*
meandering hillside
stroke the plush
refuse to pilfer.

You are a fiefdom of heavy oak
iced breath
tunneled possum
winter's bland speech.

I want to drown
my body
in pools so clear
they reflect your face.

The child across the way
cannot climb you
settles for the low bank
pitted roads
loose dirt.

Sometimes the sky is so
hazardous
she can't read your name
is unsure
how to save things.

The child under the woodpile

dines alone on dry bread, broth
swabs the snow
cares for her dog with a thick comb.

The river runs through the girl's hands
as if it is praying
thaws her blue veins.

Winter maims roofs
stencils the grass in
glass etched love notes.

The child
warms the woodpile
wants to speak in the
language of river
turn loss into an heirloom.

She deals in twin sets

double corgis
a bride and groom poised
on top of an apricot
wedding cake
places a double crib set
in the green room

remembers your body
sheened with moonlight
then vanished
beyond her fluency.

She is building an animal shelter
twin sets of each species
wants to insure longevity
propagate the pregnant

let nothing
go missing.

She bakes cake in the snow

whispers to the river
draws the mercy of water
into the broken up pebbled
pitch of her voice

wears winter in her bones
the defiled schoolgirl forced
to offer your blue assertions
a spoon-fed home.

If there are birds that hive
death in their wings
sing to the stone bridge
belled tower, fox, thistle

if she is permissioned to limp
her sloped body toward the river
listen
will she hear the silted voice
of God calling?

In her hands wander blue ponies

slips from the underworld
paw prints of rabbit, mink
slush of snow.

In her hands wander dwarf asphodel
Tibetan animals, circus acrobats
the day's foreclosures

small impasses that marry the cold.

She sits like a bent tree

forced to navigate winter
sloffs snow off her boots
takes the trail that leads to Ridge Road.
The dogs get ahead
dive into barbed bushes, tall grass
like housebound children
let loose from the misgivings
that carry us.

She has known winters like this
cramped apartments
where love hawks thin trousers
an armload of ice

and in the Northwest a cedar shake house
that ran clear down to the river
a house squandered under the
surveillance of your gaze
the way you divorce kisses
play toys, a double bed
squirrel in the absences you pave.

She watches you

from her wood pile
mink of the sleek coat
supple body, webbed feet
you who are hounded for the beauty
of your pelt as if you are industry

watches the way you trap muskrat
sweet talk rabbit, mice, move in quick
travel the current, winter
unperturbed amid the ice.

February arrives in single digits
mating season about to begin
you the prolific lover
able to swell your colony
in a scant number of years.

But are you discriminate
will there be a succession of suitors
that charm with the dazzle of their fur
offer up gift of rodent, juniper, lark
will one of them stay loyal
wait over spring's gestation
be there when the six or seven babies
arrive thin haired with closed lids ?

While you are nursing
will he bring back fish, grubs

guard you like a queen
promise never to let go

or will he be called beyond himself
ease his body into the forward thrust
of the current like a stranger
never look back?

If she shrinks small

will you sit with her
wake a vestibule of light
raked loam
the old world version
of painted cup

will she become the bell
that wafts over roofs
loosens snow
slips into dresses no longer
too big, too tight

if she shrinks small
small as a mite
will you nap in her valley
will the dogs stay patient
the pedants of elocution
resist carving a groove of rain
in the wood of her side table

will she learn to mouth words
slow, soft skinned
curved as the shape of apples
faithful
dance and spin
in her burgundy toe shoes

if she shrinks small
will she become pliable

open tongued
able to hold winter
the muskrats, mink
the you who refuses to marry her
hold steady to her course

mouth the river, rhythmic
a ground for remembering
her words the tanned ankles
of summer girls wading?

The girl has always wanted

another child
another reason to take hold
play in the snow
eat white flakes as if they are holy.
She fights nothing the river is willing
to give back
fishes with her bare hands.

January is an arm of ice so thick
roof swords dangle
the man dying of loneliness
barely manages to hoist himself up
the river turns pencil thin
as a waxed brow.

If what we counted on never comes
only the smudged windows
baseboard hissing it's angular duty
to magnify the heat

if the woman with whittled breath
who has always wanted to pregnant your love
is willing to sit long enough
weld herself to the river
wet, icy as February
shortchange nothing of the wind's fraudulence
its scarred beauty and flint vernacular

will she find in the cuff of her longing
a pale necklace that halters the dark

find a different afternoon waiting
become the language of river
leverage winter's ice
her body
into the sound, texture
clear repose
of a more ample voice calling?

Up the valley

the house with the pitched roof
holds thin light, a stenciled tree
leans a sled, dog house
blue tarped logs.

Pregnant, the girl hopes for an easy birth
loyal man, solid ring.
She is young, pretty
in love with his work boots
the strength of his hands
fingers the scarf she is making for him.
It is thick wool, brown flecked
solid as the sky.

Mid-January and the small church
up the road refuses to give up
its hourly recital of the bells
as if a prolonged birth will
someday descend on us.

The girl likes to hear the bells
finger the spindle crib
her second cousin has loaned
stir the soup thick with yams
red potato, chickpeas.

The boy's headlamps crush
the wind whipped snow.

He will be a father soon
drives anxious to get back
knows she will not ask more
than he is willing to give.

The girl leans in the slope
of her armchair
twirls wool, loops stitches
lulls in the quiet measure
of her needles clicking
has learned not to expect
what sometimes flies away.

Part Two

A Paragraph in a Sad Hotel

We weren't worried

about paying the bills
the girl down the block who
tucks her tattered slip
under the thin of her skirt
as if there is no January

weren't worried about
discontent in the side street
vanished jobs
cancer, recession
a foreclosed house.

It was winter
the sled strewn high
streets pill boxed white
mound after mound after mound
till we could erase our periled lives
ransomed summer.

We couldn't keep up with it
the snow falling
the snow falling!

After the early diagnosis

She calls it her *shrill breath sailing*
can see far off ponies
girls with blue scissors
winter storms in a pillbox

umbrellas your love
inside her snow globe
a forest of trees flexing
inside sweet rolls
early detection
marriage with more than just the
paper thin of a cigar band hosting it.

She calls it *chimney breath*
the smoke that climbs out of her mouth
twines into a cloud spiral
summer orchard
boys humming

steam presses her skirt
calls it *a gift from the highlands*
tries to spin clear, smooth as glass
so blank you can see out the other side
knows how fractured glass offends you
later will be dismissed as *too messy*
cancer coated
jagged for your finger's white purse.

She puffs breath into the January air
as if God is watching

ignores your professorial eye
that tape measures winter
makes the next and the next
and the next
your prey.

They were getting to know each other

She shows him her poems
pullet toy
miniature dance queen

watches him polish wine
his voice's treacle
make swans travel down
a radioactive canal
desolate

watches the weight
of his mind's ball field
unequivocal allegiance
to winter.

She is playing with light

its twirl and skein
wants to rework history
turn late ripened fruit into
a cellar of wealth

spins stories in your ear
calls you her *one and only*
orphaned bud
stitches paper into pages
a carefully spined book.

After a while your words
became waxed soldiers lost in
the wallpaper of other women.

A boy child travels through her
brighter than oranges
later a four-year-old girl child
arrives in a paper boat
and she knows she loves them
denser, surer than April
sings them her best orchard.

You build fence, dig holes
bury the past, her love notes
rise up on your tall horse
purvey the scenery
search a *better* landscape
extinguish what's grown old.

The air is steamy

Her eyelet burns holes
in the gutter of your voice
the snug of your arms
circling.

January divides things
dines on scant soup
never shoulders enough bread.

She forgets names, birthdays
slumps in your rutted boat
electrified ocean.

Sepia morning

She remembers once making love
along the Tootle River
off the side road of Hwy 26

her two year old boy child
napping in the back seat
your pants easy to unzip

the moss across the tree rubbing
how the damp cedar, the alder
bramble, salmonberries
took her body in
sought to become her
or was it she
who sought to become them?

It is winter

You speak professor
the pragmatics of textbook
lecture about heat displacement
air tight windows
the way bodies age past
the habit of lovemaking.

She begins to doubt her hands
lips' initiatives
pit bull her extended family
of love notes.

It is winter
the chill and bone
iced sheets, dungarees, words
poverty of the pinched river.

You tell her there is no sea
no dancing walrus
ageless lovemaking

till she half believes you
but her feet keep leaking
want to run away
from your shoes.

Vermont

She eats snow
its pearly exuberance
lets it erase pride, decibels
ambition, celebrity
bury them in mounds
that don't talk back
shotgun the field

deals in erasure
frizzle and fret
families that fall apart
get stapled back
deals in broken rooms
patient dogs
lunchboxes, ferrying

wants to nest the day
ancient vows
her children
hold it all
loose, faithful
ecclesiastic
without breaking.

She doesn't want to ride a dead pony

suffer the lost vim
sedge of you
way your hollowed carcass
bemoans a sod bed
the years of smoothing
the crease of your mane
carrying water buckets
bruised apples

doesn't want to listen any longer
to the spurn and scavenger
troll of you
way you curate words
marry luck to disaster

flirt with the farthest field
sidestep her sugar cubes.

She remembers the woods

stamped in torn chestnuts
a map of finger roots
the way you corrugated winter
wore it like a husked toy
chopped three cords of oak
suffocated the last of the green tomatoes
in a burlap sack till their skins bled.

Come December she slid cinnamon
into your mulled cider
offered up potato soup
a new language for bird pecks
called them *gift*
against your will refused to abort
the promise of her newborn.

She remembers the cottonwoods
stalwart trunks of cedar
suet tucked into bird feeders
cat's ceremonial circling
winter' gray coat
her nightly fumble with snow chains
a mile up the gravel road
excited to get back
way your voice worshiped
the even lines of the beige wallpaper

and she remembers how you wore the lust
of her body in uneven fistfuls

the lonely pregnancy
midwife at the low income clinic
tow headed miracle birth of her child

remembers the plastic
stretched taut over windows
parable of the wolves
your ship wrecked history
blue fictions

and she remembers pleading over
your late night porn, private emails
the way you nursed other women's
panty factories
over time deep grooved the wood
gutted the once generous lines
of her supper table.

In her dream she herds sheep

They are a ragged family
refuse to be rushed
over the speechless hills
stay loyal to the land, the river
marbled sky
light the day drizzles.

In her dream the ewes
nuzzle her body
distance menace
the perils of winter.
She hoists bushels
squires the fold.

For many years she lived far away
in a wet Northwest city that felt clever
on the verge of something
well lit, sanctioning
felt fraught with a much denser
silent kind of winter.
Knew love there
the kind born slippery that
relies on newness, purgatory.
There were two children
a house turned in on itself
man who slurred words
looked for other bodies
never felt bad.

The girl once lived in a cedar shake house
with a glimpse of the river
set up a child's cook stove
blue wade pool, fairy scarves
grew squash, sweet potatoes, cucumber
in the dark listened to the nutria
one solitary owl in the tree.

Now she herds sheep.
They are faithful companions
travel easy over the browned slopes
the day anoints for them

accept the uneven light, icy seasons
sky's mottled coat
turn a forgiving eye
on the world's raking.

Part Three

Uncompromised Heaven on a Shoestring

When death started to move unrelenting

in and out of her blue space
tyrant want, crayon the grass
she had to stop feeding it
weepy envelopes
milk and honey
stop carrying it in buckets
that outweigh the rain.

When death started to move
in and out of her showy places
canker the rapt allegiance of roses

she called out the April of your name
as if the greening of your river
could be enough.

You dark loom her body
swallow death down
like a bird with a whistle
in its throat
heaven on a shoestring.

It was done

she knew that
the finality of her heart
cruel eye of lovers
who cigarette burn holes
snowball the dark
for needing them.

It is the year of loss
shot gunned kittens
a threadbare couch

the *she* born of the sycamore tree
who swoons past winter
wants to marry the moon's bare legs.

She stick stirs the river

into a blue eddy
remembers her mother
in the skimpy kimono
shoveling the drive as if
lust can live past diligence.

What if happiness is absent minded
takes more than it gives
flaunts good legs, an appetite
surfeit of stuff
while the dark seeps

what if happiness is fickle
as the world's love
and she is left forlorn
frost flecked, newly anointed
inside the quiet disaster of things

will she still be able to hear
God's holy voice calling?

You navigate her heart

like a pull toy
don't speak cruel.

She skates on ice so thin
it can barely carry her
sleeps with the snow
survives winter's cramped fist

campfires her hips
inside the secret fluency
of your deeper burning.

You mouth her words

travel them slow, rhythmic
as if all things are memory
and forgetting

mouth them faithful as
the tanned ankles of
summer girls wading
the wind beyond corruption

mouth her words unencumbered
as girls who drink death down
vouchsafe the lives
apprenticed to their table

who late night, wordless
slip away
down the embankment
discard their blued dresses

float silent, moon crazed
inside the predictable love
the river's clear eye
gives back.

The months of winter

She wasn't fence proofing the past
into a blue notebook that
never speaks dirty

but still the weight of the cold
season of cheap lunchmeat
interminable gray
accumulates.

To paddle in this snow
she must make herself porous
lean on the scent of pine
scarce love notes.

Whoever takes this road
is warned of a bone chill
decimated roses
cereal version of happiness
that stalks houses.

To drink from this cup
she must marry the wind
promise everything
be willing to worship
the color of death towing.

She lives in your shroud and wake

learns to jump flame
take the bane out of words
travel a sod cottage
three flushed children.
The cat stops massacring red wings.

She grows wild orchid
star of Bethlehem
sweet talks the trees
the river's blue jesus
with her ravaged silk
thawed body

mixes her spit with loam
poultices her lover
heals his penchant
for looting.

Mustela Vison

soon your long sleek body, webbed toes
will travel up and down the embankment
sweet talk the body's blue velvet.
It is February, almost mating season.
There will be many suitors.

Late spring when the crocus flirt
along the wind's armpit
you will give birth to a handful of babies
nurse and cradle with their eyes shut

stalked for your sleek pelt
will peril your life
in the consummate
act of lovemaking.

In winter

she fries turnip
eats potato soup piqued with ginger
deals card games
sings *The Bally Ho of Dunmartin*.
Suet shines on the face of her bread.

Tucked in thick boots, mittens
she goes out, licks the snow
your braille, hard surfaces

forgives the dark
for so much loss.

Are all roads good roads

will she know love by a handshake
the way your sod cleaves
the loyalty of her pear trees
how they puddle fruit
even after summer's thin rain?

Will she recognize you by touch
your voice, the way your words
field ice, chapel February
set to rest the terrible uncertainty
of her bed

will she sleep easy with you
recognize you by the light you lend
way you brush the fur of animals
wash words
till they are earth scented
an uncluttered room
women who gather the grain
worship the snow?

She is entering a castle

marooned velvet
dusty filigree
mahogany chairs
obligatory dogs
fires that persist
warm their guests
past nightfall

has brought her deft slippers
showgirl stockings
broken vows
armloads of loss
thick as death
thick as the snow falling

no longer in the hope
somebody else
will want to marry her.

Part Four

The Quiet Disaster of Things

She has scalded hands

healed over
doesn't want to speak cruel
mark the snow with her burns.
It is the season of the epiphany
no name saying
the river icy
underneath a catalog of motion.

She knows things disappear –
the body's prayer book
children, home, family
knows she has scalded hands
missionary hope
asks the god of sawn limbs
for mercy.

It is the beginning of January
the sun no tyrant in the eastern sky
the weekend visitors hauling skis
snow shoes, poles
her hands itchy inside the gloves
till the river decides to claim them
swallows her right up
and she is gone.

In the sleepy hollow of Braithwaite

it became a legend of sorts
when the strange girl departed
left nothing of her woodpile
but a scrap of lace.

Some folks believe St. Christopher
patron saint of hard shoed travelers
lured her, spoke the dharma of the road
salmonberries, blue thistle

still others claim a pack of wolves
turned greedy, left blood in the snow
her scarf snagged on a tree limb

still others swear that Angus, the baker
shooed her away after his prize tartlets
day old loaves went missing

and still others, a small straggle of them
believe she had grown weary of wintering
fled this world of her own volition

what is known is that the girl
who buried herself in hoarfrost, feldspar
was never seen again slouched over her flame
tooling words into the bent ear of animals

that her life changed course that day
bade *fairwell* to the miller's red barn
fairwell to the butcher, the Collier Inn
bake shop

as if a different tune played in her ear
as if some peculiar night bird
had swooped in to carry her.

All that is known is that on the 8th of January
two winters ago under the guise of a pale moon
in the season of our Lord's holy epiphany
a strange girl went missing

that at the Tibbett and O'Malley farm
sheep fell silent in the field
and the town's almighty woodpile
fell down in a freak wind.

All we can hope is that
the girl's scalded hands, voice
grew back new
married her
clear and loyal as the river calling.

No wooden marker

signals her grave
no timbrels, drum roll
plastic roses
blue lipped homily.

The girl in the woodpile
with her dog, oyster shells
Tibetan animals
escaped down the river
of forgetfulness

grew so soft, permeable
even the night
unpinned its voice
stopped snatching.

Townspeople
willed back new limbs
unbent the weight of their coats
blessed their neighbor
potatoes, leeks

that greener landscape
beyond the dark's imperialism.

Part Five

Blue Halo

For how many years

did she listen
to his voice's dust coat
as if she must patronize
tout his holy grail
weave hard propositions
into Christmas?

No longer the policed precinct
girl slung on a stick
now she cleaves to honeycombs
the garden's processional
spins in her excess

dances the dead weight of things
turns the white earth
hard north
into snow people.

You spot clean winter

write on her
till ruddy skinned
she is able to amble
your secret inlets
savor the long pause

become the flashlight
that orchards the dark
leaves room
always leaves room

lets your celestial
wander her blue halo.

For you

she floats the secret language of river
picnics on a blue tarp
mascaras the snow

for you she lays out soda crackers
soup, pecan cheese
lets the drifts eat her

for you she dabs up her past
no longer snowballs

is buried in white
a call girl bride
slew of cake

your nameless
kind of death calling.

There are furrows of blue bells

in the far field
they sing for her
press their lips skyward
as if god is listening.

Do you remember the dress
mud stained
splashed in the fade of lilac
the way her body leaned
past Shrove Thursday
and into the sloped field
torched your midnight
with a bold kiss?

How long to demolish winter
its mangled rooms
rock salted road
eat up the snow
become a softer filament
unwaxed flirtation?

She brushes her hair
one hundred strokes
for one hundred guppies
brushes the frozen path
to your door.

The retrieval of winter

When the thawed ice
is willing to marry her
when she slugs then twirls
wedded to thick wool
mud boots, the rutted road
wedded to a joy that keeps watch
over the hills
hangs out in sandwich shops
on park benches
forgets the coin feed laundry, damp wood

when you come with your scuffed cowboy boots
stories of spice merchants, shipwrecks
exotic birds
your willingness to easy over the eggs
stir-fry the vegetables
listen to the palaver of her uneven sweet-talk
willingness to please

when you knock the snow off her heels
soft stroke the dogs
begin to announce the tender in her
refuse to complain about the dimming

don't say that littered with the past's
hard winter
she will turn away.

Thank you for loving

All night she kisses your neck
your thighs
secret interstices
sleeps in the juice of you
listens to soft vowels
wind in the trees
does not run away

all night odd kingdoms arrive
defenseless
the catechism of the dark sings
she practices praise
rolls it on her tongue like
the good witch who deflects spiteful

all night the sheets threaten to burn
the city of larks stays faithful
animals forgive our rancor
hold to your splash of stars
forest as home.

She twines ribbon

banners the street, her voice
into loose April
fashions her brightest lips

slips into an eyelet dress
that seeps sunlight
doesn't want to map her scared child
woman you with so many kisses
you turn blue as the ocean.

It is the day of her wedding.
There are trays of pie
roasted turnip, beets
hand basins to rinse
the soot of the road.

Small birds feed.
She sponges the white of your skin
washes the cup of you
forgives the wind
for snatching.

She wears silky stockings

mud boots
pockets stones
pussies the moon

turns paw print, twig
into lamplight
for the blue girl

letterpresses
his words
files the cruel out

courts the day
in the mute language
of snow falling.

Part Six

The Bells

Who says the angels must

beg for their bread
the city wears only shabby shoes
impervious to the decency
of snow falling?

There are treacherous roads.
They take practiced navigation
map reading.
People have perished
palsied their heart.
But still the deer, possum arrive
seasons of jonquil, lupine, fairy slipper
the determination to hold joy
even amidst the frenzy.

Who says the angels must
barb the past
aim balls so rock hard
they banish winter
leak coal into the girl's nightdress.

January mutes light
speaks the retinol of buried things
snow falling faster than she can carry it.

Sometimes nothing makes sense
the angels must wait
windows ice up
the dog forgets
the kisses she once traveled him

every word she once knew
becomes a fleur-de-lis
algorithm of loss
tease and tell
where her body must once again
relearn its ample geography.

It is not unusual for the angels
to sit up late night
weave us a tapestry of leftovers
sedge, spilt tea, slimed oats
parlay want into a foot stool
so delicate, forlorn, speechless
it outlasts the cold.

In the ordinary course of her days

how does she explain
place sensible words to it
this desire that runs so deep, so crazy
full of berm and thistle
candle and calamine
it escapes the banks of the river
flows forceful even now
toward the sea

explain how love moves
beyond the downed limbs, deadfall
weeps over our distances
knows the past can't harm
not his airtight words
spewed epitaphs
the way his heart squeezed her breath
like a snake devouring whole
the body of the road kill
that she is more than the disused shoe
bothersome weed

how does she explain
understand from love to love
the way life holds a steady gaze
our words get unrobed
by a softer midnight

the way true lovers keep
the memory of snow
as if even amid barbed wire
there remains the height of the trees
embrace of the river?

She slides into her amber coat

the one that never walks away
shrill in a windstorm.

The pond has frozen.
The frogs fled.
She cannot will back spring
thaw the ice speckled fields
holds a secret ambition
writes your holy name on her lips.

January stalks thin bone
drifts of snow.
She eats porridge, two bowls.
Her amber coat fits.
No longer two sizes too big
two sizes too small.

She is traveling without skates
slips her hands into mittens.
They are green over brown wool
made by the sheepherder hands
of her mother.

Everywhere the girl sees you
amber her field
puncture the still air
hour upon hour
with the tremble of the bells.

Toni Thomas lives in Portland, Oregon. Her poems have been published in Austria, Spain, New Zealand, Canada, England, Scotland, and Australia. In the United States her work has appeared in over fifty literary magazines including *Prairie Schooner, North Dakota Quarterly, Hayden's Ferry Review, the Minnesota Review, Notre Dame Review, Poetry East,* and more. She has been twice nominated for a Pushcart prize, and won several awards. She has published twenty-two collections of poetry and six books for children.

Her figurative clay sculptures have been shown in gallery exhibits in Portland and Chicago, displayed in literary magazines, and housed in private collections in the U.S. and England.

Her short documentary *One of Us* was shown at the Trans-ideology: Nostalgia festival in Berlin and at the Museum of Contemporary Art in Taipei.

Since Toni loves to create and sits buried in reams of poems, manuscripts, clay figures and images....she likes to imagine all of them out in the world
swaying wild as the lupine.

tonithomaspoetry.com

www.ingramcontent.com/pod-product-compliance
Lightning Source LLC
Chambersburg PA
CBHW060621080526
44585CB00013B/934